*For the love of
a woman*

ISBN 978-0-6151-3574-8
Copyright © 2006 by Matthew Lohr
All rights reserved

Table of contents

A New Rose	1
My Fantasy	5
Lady	9
Untitled	13
Sophisticated Behavior	17
End of times	23
The perfect day	27
For the love of a woman	29
Tribal Spirit	33
Till I come home	37
What if	39
Wait and See	41
Get Here	45
Happy Mother's Day	49
Lover's Play	53
Forever	57
In the distance	61
Woman	65
The journey	67
Through your smile	71
Serenity	77
The seed of the prophet	81
Love to fly	83
Déjà vu	87
Loving her	91
Will you	95

A New Rose

Like a new rose opening on its first dawn
The sun's rays glistening off the petals in the early morn
The stem is your pedestal giving you sustenance
Displaying your beauty the sun's only reason for existence
No baby's breath
Definitely no vase
They only hide your beauty
And smother your grace
I praise the air you breathe
The land on which you stand
And when you blossom
It's more than I can stand
They say a life spent looking for the perfect bloom
Is not a life wasted
So every time you walk in the room

I'm glad I spent the time
And know my time
Was well spent
Because this find is so fine
Many men
Spend
Time looking for diamonds and platinum
And I just look at them
And try not to laugh at them
Because even though the diamond shines
For a long time
It's just sits there while the rose grows with the sunshine
They praise the diamond
But it's called ice 'because it's cold
And I'd rather bask in the warmth
That your beauty holds
So as I watch
Your pedals unfold
I realize I found more riches
Then diamonds, platinum, and all the gold
That's been stole
But they can't steal what I see
Because I love the vision
Of the beauty within thee

And I watch the pedals
As they gently fall
To the ground I pick them up
And choose to save them all
People don't understand why
I want to spend the rest of my life with thee
It's simple after seeing your grace I realize
I was already blessed with
The most beautiful site there is to see

My Fantasy

Can't you see
You're my fantasy
Cause this is exactly
Where I want to be
Playing with your hair
As we cuddle
In the easy chair
Watch TV by the fire
While the kids sleep upstairs
It's been a long hard week
But I don't even care
We need no words to speak
As long as in your eyes I get to stare

I spent so many lonely nights
Before you entered my life
So I had to ask
Would you be my wife?
I must be blessed
Because you said yes
Without a second thought
And put my worries to rest
Filled a hole in my soul
Gave me reasons to smile
Carried my seed
And blessed me with a child
So I don't roam
The streets I come home
Quick to be in the midst
Of your love zone
Your skin tone
Simply turns me on
And I love nothing more
Than waking up with you at dawn
I don't mind the rainy days
Cause you are my sun
And in a crowded room
You're still the only one
I see
 You're my fantasy

I'm the envy of many
With my perfect life
The best kids
With my perfect wife
I'll travel the highest mountain to the
Deepest sea to give you the perfect pearl
Because I have
The perfect world
And there's no place
I'd rather be
Except right here
With my fantasy
The reality is
You're just my fantasy
Cause I don't know you
And you certainly don't know me
There's no house
With no easy chair
No fire place
No kids to sleep upstairs
Cause you're nothing to me
Except a silly fantasy
And I just imagine
The way things could be

Which makes me think?
Could I possibly be?
Your silly
Fantasy

Lady

So sexy and shapely
Got me thinking lately
For you to cross my path
 Is either a blessing or fate see
You know I'm in love
With your brown skin
Love the feeling I get
Whenever we're down in
Our own world holding you
Got you next to me
Your voice so soft so silky
Just like sex to me
Pure ecstasy
You know I can't wait to be
With you touch you kiss you
Oh how I hate to be

Alone in this world
Negativity all in the scene
A man's home is his castle
But it's empty without a queen
So I try to live
Every day like its valentines
And wonder if you can find
It in your heart to be mine
Cause I have plans for you
You know I'm the man for you
So I strive every day
Just to understand you
The best part of you
Isn't for my eyes to be seeing
Because I'm in love
With the very essence of your being
These men who
Think their god's gift to women
To appreciate your beauty
They aren't even beginning
They have it all wrong
But I'm not mad at them
They just forgot that
God gave Eve to Adam

And he gave you to me
So my soul you could help uplift
And I'm here to tell you
I'm in love with my gift

Untitled

Loving you and not knowing
How you feel makes me so sick
Like Ne(-y)o straight up
I'm all caught up in your matrix
The plain and simple truth is
My feelings are neither plain nor simple
Because I don't know if I love the sound of you voice
Or your smile and dimples
Or maybe
It's the way that you say hey baby
That drives me crazy
And keeps my vision so hazy
That's too simple
So it has to be the way that you say
All the things you say
That makes me want to listen to you every day

I don't even remember
When I first began to love you
I know
It's not the first chance I go to hug you
In fact I'm sure
That it came some time after
See I remember you laughter
During all our phone chit chatter
Does it even matter?
No not if you don't feel the same
Living with that part
Is what drives me insane
But the pain is eased
Whenever I see your smile
It lights up the room
And simply drives me wild
And the light fades to dusk
Whenever you leave
And you're not with me
That part I choose not to believe
So I hang on to my fantasy
Because it has to be
'Cause if I spill my reality
Then it's catastrophe

So maybe

I'll accept one more kiss on the cheek

We can share a drink

Say our goodbyes and not have to speak

Sophisticated Behavior

I have sophisticated tastes
For sophisticated flavors
Only the finest delicacies
Do I put to my lips to savor
Exotic dishes from
The far corners of the earth
But none of this
Can determine my worth
I may dress in high fashion
From exclusive boutiques
Francias et Italienne
Just some of the languages I speak
But one day
From the corner of my eye
I can't deny
She looked fly

My composure slipped

I tried to recover quick

But I felt this

Twitch in my lips

My throat became dry

And somewhat parched

My fine clothes began to itch

Maybe from too much starch

My mind began to wander

Thoughts became uneasy

Sophistication was lost

Because your grace amazed me

My tie tightened

Like a noose around my neck

As I started to lose

All my self respect

I felt hypnotized

And I don't know why

Yet suddenly your beauty

Brought a tear to my eye

So I thought to say hello

But my mind said no

And for some reason my feet

Just wouldn't let me go

Now I'm thinking
Roses in a dozen
I need to back my mind off
Thinking about her lovin
See for her to be here
In my space and time
Makes me think that the planets
Have perfectly aligned
She's my star that shines
Turning night to daytime
Easing my stress
Turning work to play time
I'm sorry I think
I lost my sophistication
Cause she has me feeling
Pent-up frustrations
See my fascination
With her presence and poise
Drives my poetry and prose
And she's my only choice
Now my sophisticated side has me
Planning to say something clever
Yet the simple sight of her
And those words just never
Ever seem to materialize

My brain cells scatter
For the life of me
I really don't know what's the matter
Because there might be
I mean just slightly
And outside chance that
She actually likes me
When she walks away she
Takes 3 steps turns back and smiles
And I've already said
That just drives me wild
So I lose control
Reach for her hand to hold
And damn my feet
By themselves start to stroll
Towards her and my neck
Starts to sweat from the heat
She looks so perfect
I say that we need to speak
She says ok
Kisses my cheek and walks away
And I must admit I like
The way her skirt sways
So I don't really mind
But then my mind
Loses track of all
Space and time and I'm

Scrambling to find my
Sophisticated self
Regain my composure
And hope that no one else
Noticed my feeble attempts
At trying to flirt
Or when I strained to
Keeps my eyes from her shirt
The surge of my primal urges
For her natural flavor
Wait a minute let me stop
Please excuse my unsophisticated behavior

End of times

Stormed tossed currents
Over the ocean's great depths
Ice covered mountain peaks
On long Himalayan treks
Tornadoes across the plains
Earthquakes splitting the land
Hurricane's devastation
Make many fear what is at hand
Volcanic eruptions
Reshaping the earth
Forest fires stripping away
Mother Nature's worth
Typhoons and monsoons
Wreak havoc on populations
Famine and disease
Destroying many nations

Tsunami's wiping
Away costal villages and towns
Sink holes pulling
People's entire world underground
Floods seem
To wash away people's dreams
Leaving many to wonder
What all of this means
Disasters of many kinds
Have many people's minds
Wondering if these are signs
Of the coming of the end of times
The Mayan calendar
Ending in 2012
Has people wondering
How to save them selves
Since the beginning
Mystics have predicted the end
So to me
There's nothing really new in this trend
The day of reckoning
May be at hand
And destruction may
Be coming to wipe out the land

It's been said many times
And if it's true
I'm blessed in these times
To have met an angel like you

The perfect day

It was the day
I awoke with a smile on my face
The windows open
A tropical breeze cooled the place
The day I learned
To speak with my mouth wide shut
I looked up
And the heavens opened up
An angel came to sit
Right here on my shoulder
The day all days got brighter
And the nights no longer any colder
The day I first saw
A perfect sunset
The day I'll never forget
That's the day we first met

For the love of a woman

For the love of a woman
I sit here and wait
Patiently see
I cleared my slate
My to do list
Has long been completed
So like a kid in class
I try to be quiet and remain seated
I did all the homework
And read all of the lessons
Memorized all the answers
So for me there's no guessing
I'm not stressing yet
The love of a woman makes
Me lie in my bed
Late at night wide awake

Staring at the ceiling
Thinking about these feeling
I have and I laugh at myself
Because my heart needs healing
See there a hole
That's in there still
That only
The love of a woman can fill
I don't mean to be
So emotionally strung
But it's like I have been
Climbing a ladder and can't reach the last rung
Like I have been running a race
But just can't find the finish
Like the candles don't get bright
The light only seems to diminish
Empires rise and fall
And start new beginnings
Wars are fought and lost
For the love of women
I've studied everything
From Ars amoria
To the Kamasutra
I hope I'm not boring you

It's not for me but
So I know how to love her
Touch and kiss her
Massage caress and simply how to hug her
I pay attention to how
My mother is loved by my father
And realize I can never
Tell a woman I can't bother
Never tell her that
I simply haven't the time
Never treat her like
I'm not blessed just because she's mine
So when she's with me
I'll treat her as my queen
And let her know
She's more beautiful than any actress on a screen
Her very breath
Breathes life into my soul
The sight of her
Is more precious then gold
More valuable than diamonds
More beautiful than a rose
Her elegance flows
From a source no one knows

The no treasure more sought after
So I have cleaned my slate
And for the love of a woman
I'll continue to wait

Tribal Spirit

Try to stay calm
My blood starts to run
Pumping through my veins
Heart beats like a tribal drum
Soul shakes like a tribal dance
Words spoken like a tribal chant
Possessed but no longer repressed
Thoughts expressed through my idle trance
Can't control the flow
It's like a spiritual ritual
Can't tear my self away
From the addiction it's habitual
It tears down my inhibitions
Inhibits my reflexes
My reaction to this attraction
Seems as natural as that of the sexes

Opposite ends pulling together
Forever tugging in the same direction
The tribal spirit pulling me
Into the unknown yet what happens next in
The midst of tribal celebrations
Has me thinking about nation
Building tensions building rebuilding
Visions of the beginning of creation
Sensations pulling me closer into
The heat of the tribal fire
Sweat on my brow getting hotter
Matching the intensity of my burning desire
Flames burning higher
Still higher till I only see
Fire consuming me
Realizing the flame comes from within me
Now all I see
Is the tribal spirit looking at
Me drawing me
In so close I can't turn back
So I surrender to the spirit
Let the spirit take control
It inhales my mind,
My body and dominates my soul

Become one with the spirit
Yes it all that's left to do
I no longer fear the spirit
Because the tribal spirit is you

Till I come home

It's true
I still think of you
Last saw you years ago
What am I to do
I remember all the gifts
We exchanged at Christmas
And every December 25th
It's your face that I miss
Every Valentine
I still feel that you mine
Though the sun in the spring time
No longer seems to shine
Summer cookouts on
Our old favorite grill
Think it has the same
Coals from our last cookout still

I just keep hanging on
Though I know that you're gone
But you don't have to worry
Because you know that I'm strong
Your soul keeps me warm
Because your love is so real
I still light the dinner candles
And enjoy our favorite meal
Fall asleep on the couch
By the firelight
Haven't slept in the bed
Since we shared our last night
Get out the old box of pictures
So I can see your lovely face
Imagine you walking in the room
And the way you lit up the place
Read all of your old letters
It's all I have to do
Till god calls me home
And I can get right back to you

What if

What if I had butterflies?
And there's something I couldn't say
Because it's been a long time
Since someone so wonderful looked my way
What if every time you kissed my cheek
I wish it was closer to my lips
What if every time I caught a flight
I wish you could make the trip
Now don't get me wrong
I mean I'm happy that we're friends
And if it never changes from this
I'll be happy from now until the end
But what if it was more
And I said mi amore you're the one I adore
And I stood up and took the chance
To show you all of what I have in store

So what if I said all of this
Would you stay and listen or just walk away
And what if I wrote this in a letter
Would you read till the end or just throw it away
Now what if this what if
Really isn't just some old what if
Because every time I hear your voice
I can feel your tenderness
And what if we both laughed
And agreed this wouldn't work
And I said you should be honest
Because my feelings wouldn't be hurt
Could we still be the friends?
We are right here and now
Or what if you felt the same
Could we make the leap I'll show you how?
Or what if this is all too much
And now you wish it would end
Either way I'm glad I wrote this
Because I'm blessed I can call you my friend

Wait and See

Fascination, joy and elation
Just some of the sensations
That I get whenever I view
God's most beautiful creation
My mind's fixation
My soul's orientation
Has my train arriving
Right here at your station
Is it my final destination?
That part's not really clear
But we can take a slow walk in your garden
As long as we're here
We can stay and play
Till the day fades away
At night I can look in your eyes by the moonlight
Till the sunlight takes it away

Now your body makes me fiend
But I'm not just trying to get in your jeans
I want the two of us to grow
And I want to know all of your child hood dreams
You more beautiful than a rose
And I can see you've been scorned
So let me just hold you and appreciate your beauty
See I can handle the thorns
It's nothing that I
Really haven't seen before
Because my heart to
Bears the scars of loves war
But you and I
We can start a new era
And you have me hypnotized
So forgive me if I stare a
Bit, at those hips, that you switch
Even when you just stand
Come here
And let me make you understand
That I'm a man and I
Can be satisfied with a tender kiss and hug
Or we can walk down by the lake
And make beautiful love

And then you'll see
How you and me
Can make one or three
Or more if you choose to be
With me
Make a family
Whatever you want I guess we
Will have to just wait and see

Get Here

I know we
Argued yesterday and all night
Had our biggest fight
You couldn't stand the sight
Of me
I didn't want to see you anyway
My friends say
Man you don't need her anyway
I want you to see
Just how angry you make me
Feel my angst
As I feel it but don't hate me
My feelings wouldn't be slighted
If I didn't feel for you in the first
And I still feel the same
So for what its worth that's why it hurts

But the argument was yesterday
And today is a new day
So I need you to come
Around my way so I can say
I love you
Though you hurt my feelings
And I probably hurt yours
Can we start our healing?
We can be like
Two kids in a sandbox
Cause next week
We both forgot who it was who knocked
The other's castle down
Just turn around and build another
You need a shovel
Well see I have another
If you're tired there's
Room in my castle for thee
And I hope you have
Room in your castle for me
I don't want to leave
The lights on so please come
Inside so I can
Turn them off and we can come

Together as one
Person one flesh one human being
Your beauty is
The only reason I have eyes to be seeing
So please let's stop
This war of words the war of the worlds
Is what this feels like?
I can't lose my only girl
And understand I
Need to know I'm your only man
And lasting love
Is our one and only plan
So get here me
Need you here no right here
So there's no space
Between us not even atmosphere
I want to hear
Your heartbeat in sync with mine
And arguments
Are just small blinks in time
And this time
That we choose to spend together
Can last forever
As long as we just share forever

So if it's by sailboat

Tree swinging rope to rope

Sled sliding down the slope

Into my arms or riding speedy colts

Crossing the border in a

Blaze of hope just get here

I need you here now

So I don't care how just get here

Happy Mother's Day

From the day
You chose for me to be
You chose to see in me
What no other could see
When I slipped
Every time you were there
For every silly thing I tried
You cared
You loved me
When I couldn't love in return
Taught me love should be given free
And that it couldn't be earned
When I was dead wrong
You stood right by my side
And through the
Look in your eyes I felt shame inside

Made me stand up
And accept the blame
Taught me that
In admitting fault there is no shame
When I tried to break away
Too early you wouldn't release
And when my heart
First broke you picked up every piece
You helped define in me
Exactly what a parent should be
So when my daughter does wrong
And I wonder what the punishment should be
Her sad eyes look at me
And it's so hard and I just get so far
Before I remember love
Can be hard but it shouldn't leave scars
See I have the memory
Of just how I grew to be
A man and
I judge that by knowing you're proud of me
So that makes it
Easy for me to hold my head high
And know my dreams
Can always be pie in the sky

When I reach high

I know you would never let me fall

So I just dust

Myself off and stand tall

You're responsible

For the best in me

Made me see

Exactly what the best could be

Your love

Was, is and always will be home to me

Without your love

I wouldn't be here today

To say

I love you mom, Happy Mother's day

Lover's Play

As I close my eyes
I can barely see the ground a million miles below
And you and I
Go to a place no one else can know
Where we can't be seen
But our romance is felt
And the ice of the ages
Begins to melt
As we kiss touch and caress
Bodies start flexin
We can rock the waves
Send the tide in a new direction
Cause tsunamis
With our seismic actions
Realign the planets
With our opposite magnetic attraction

Satisfaction

Has never been this satisfying

And when face with the facts

It's true there's no denying

That you

Are the axis on which my world spins

And the constant motion

Makes it hard to breathe in

And out as I gasp for air

Our lungs collapse

As you and I

Begin to follow our own tracks

Repeat these acts

Feel the desire burn within

As we come together

Only to begin again

To the same destination

With new ways to get there

See new sights reach new heights

Taking hours to get there

I wanna kiss your neck

And caress your back

Lay in a river named after us

Getting our energy back

Ready for the second act
Of this lovers play
As it starts lights out
Night turns to day
As the sun rises
Sets in the afternoon sky
Feeding off of our love
As the two of us lie
In the fields of ecstasy
As birds sing the glory of us
And only mother nature
Can comprehend the story of us
So as the flowers bloom
And butterflies take first flight
And day turns to dusk
From your eyes I still see light
Emanating from the passion
Burning deep in your soul
And your beauty
Is almost too much to behold
So into you
I begin to sink again
With the soft smooth
Silkiness of your skin

I slip and slide
Up yet still higher
And we rekindle
These coals back into fire
Flames so high
They outshine the stars
The moon's set ablaze
And the world seems so far
So hold me now
As I take you to new depths
Let yourself go
No need to catch your breath
Because I
Will breath bliss into you
As we make
One moment into two
And two souls
Back into one
As our love
Raises us into the sun
So the whole world
Can see us in a new day
As we begin
To write a new lover's play

Forever

The amount of time
I spend thinking of you
The amount of time
That I have to love you
This time is time
That never ends
In which the hour glass
Automatically turns to begin again
I don't remember
First loving you
But it seems
It was since life was new
Before the land
Was separated from the sea
Before light was created
For one to see

I believe you
Are the first sight I ever saw
When my eyes
Were still young and raw
The lord created beauty
By placing you on earth
And through you
To love he gave birth
So before the beginning
Of the counting of time
The world had light
Simply because you shine
And ever since
Days come with no end
And nights are filled
With star lights that lend
Hope to dreams
That you will be seen again
And that in you
Love can be born again
So time will never end
And the clock will never strike
Twelve so twelve bells
Will never sound midnight

So as long

As the days have gone on

I long for you

Though some see it as wrong

For you

I will wait right here

Till the day

I have your love near

So as the pages

Of time keeping being filled

My heart

Keeps on standing still

For another

It will never beat

Until we create

The pit patter of little feet

Until then

My heart strings remained severed

And for you

I shall wait forever

In the distance

I watch as you stare
Off to places far away
Thinking of different people
Or maybe a whole new day
So I wonder
That if in these places
You imagine friendly
Or new and different faces
Is the sun shining
Or is it romantic nights
Do you have penthouse views
Or is it nature sights
Your mind seems so
Preoccupied that I feel
That the place unknown
Might hold a love so real

Or could it be
A painful memory
Of feeling you hoped
Had washed out to the sea
Do you daydream
Of carnival rides and clowns
Or remember being a child
As the merry go round and round
Looking at you
Makes my mind wander
Into fantasies
And situations to ponder
Or maybe you
See me and are in thought
Of my looks of longing
And we're both are caught
Up in this game
Imagining the dreams of others
Seeing people in the park
Wondering if their lovers
Or could you be dreaming
Of me being in your dreams
Having dreams of
Me fulfilling your dreams

I mean
Can we both have a dream
Of the same reality
Of living life as a dream
I sit here and wonder
As I
Stare and catch
The look in your eye
Thinking that
You and I
Could be more
Than two people just passing by
So as you leave
A tear comes to my eye
Thinking I never got to know you
And now we part ways
Without saying goodbye

Woman

As nature
Reveals itself so naturally
I begin to believe
That I may actually
Be witnessing nature
As it was intended to be
And feel blessed that this sight
Was intended for me
As I witness
The plains yet unblemished
And the ocean
With rivers replenished
Either way I look
I see two mountains
Separated by valleys
With just one fountain

From which
All eternity flows
Two roots
Upon which all life grows
You may see the countryside
That grows across the earth
But I see woman
From which life was given birth

The Journey

I have sat with a pen full of ink
Empty pages and thoughts of you
And I begin to drain the ink
By filling the pages I'm in another space with you
As I escape the world
In which I have been forced to live
Traveling faster than light
In this vessel of love I have to give
It makes no stops
Because you are already here
And we can go as fast as you want
As long as I get to keep you near
These trips through the universe
Are just like the first
Steps I took as a child
Setting foot on the earth

Because in each step we take

I find excitement

And I hold on tight to you

Because this road might get

A little rough but you

Steady the journey like you steady my soul

And it seems my arms were made to hold

You and take away the cold

So winter nights for us

Hold no chill

And we have no need

For fire to build and I will

Stay with you in the day

And when the nights are grey

We need no stars

Our love will navigate the way

And if we drift off course

We're still not lost

Because we have found ourselves in each other

And if the storms begin to toss

The seas I

Still have you next to me

And I fear no end

Because if it has to be

As long as you
Are still with me
Then I have truly
Lived out my fantasy

Through your smile

I was looking at your smile
And I got to thinking
I haven't seen that much style in awhile
And you just sit there blinking
Batting your eyes
Looking demure and just licking
Your lips it's almost sick
The way the air just thickens
Gets hotter the room gets smaller
But yet this empty space between us
Just gets bigger
Though I have already seen us
Standing hand in hand
On pink beaches our toes in the sand
Roaming like explorers
Yes we're discovering new lands

Creating new music with
Bass tones unknown to our own tempo
Lost in the piano keys
My heart races yet the pace is kept slow
We have both been here before
But it feels like the first
Because those other times
Are never better than our worst
Because at our worst
We are still in heaven
While others are counting the stars
We are counting the sevens
Hearing bells for weddings
With seven hundred and seventy seven place settings
Your dress as white as the angels
Can only mean that we're getting
Ready to create
Twelve new tribes of Judah
We're just two individuals
And people don't understand what we do to
Keep this bond everlasting
Foundation unshakeable
Once we became one
Our love became unbreakable

Your strength

Take the stress of the day away

And gives me strength

To take your heartache away

You have set my soul free

And my heart on fire

Deep inside of me

You fan the flames of desire

To the heights of ecstasy

We go in a carriage for two

And though everything must come down

We never seem to

Just step up

To the next plateau

Our love is as steady

As the ancient springs that flow

We'll rewrite ancient texts

On how to make love

See the heavens open

Hear the angels sing from above

Speak in tongues

While our lungs collapse

We'll die and be reborn

Through our simple acts

Of passion
Showing compassion as has been never seen
Rewrite the songs of Solomon
Create love scenes never before seen
In pictures
Or read in texts by Rhoades scholars
I am a slave
To your love your heart is my collar
So we rise and fall as one
And the beat of the drum
Is our hearts
As they beat together as one
As my sun
I revolve around you like the earth
Experiences of intimacy
Between you and me have given birth
To artists
Trying to capture our feeling with a brush
But no matter how large the canvas
There is just never enough
Paint or colors
To capture all of the sensation
Because a painter
Can only have one position he's placing

Us in and by that time
We have finished all sixty-four
Of the kamasutra
And already creating some more
So we have a door
With no handles that have locks with no keys
Though the peep hole
People see us both on our knees
Because we
Worship the blessings of our love to grow
Sharing a space and time
That no other can see understand or know

Serenity

I don't need to look to the sky
For god no more
Because he just sent
His most perfect angel to walk through my door
So I rejoice
In the blessings she brings
And recognize her voice
As the lead when all the angels sing
So I humbly accept
This gift I have been given
And see through dark skies
The sun has arisen
It is for her
That I have been wanting for sure
And through her
My needs are satisfied and I want no more

She has unlocked my dreams
And from my chains she has released
Taken away all remains of pains
Drained my despair to be replaced with peace
In her arms
I feel like I rest in the clouds
So her praises
I speak each one aloud
And when my voice fails
I begin to write these lines as her gospel
To be added to the bible
So there are no myths of her to dispel
So I show faith through works
As acts of repaying
My debt to her which I have incurred
And it goes without saying
I can never repay her
For the love I have seen through her
Because though she entered my life
Only recently I feel I knew her
At my conception
Yet that recollection is unclear
Because I am so far from where I was
Yet she has always felt near

So I will hold
Onto to her until time ends
And pray
For all of this to just begin again
Knowing that when it does
I'll repeat my actions verbatim
So these stories of us
As a prophet I'll relate them
So she
Will come back in my arms again
And this time
I will love her truer and deeper and when
Congregations are addressed
With eulogies of me
They can say through her he
Finally found serenity

The seed of the prophet

It's hard to behave
When I'm thinking about drinking the juices god gave you
And why I give your body worship and praise
To me it's simply because god made you
And from what I can see
He makes nothing less than perfection
And he made us want the same
Yet opposite so we can make this perfect connection
And I think he waited to create some things
Until he had seen us
Because some things on this planet
Can only be described by what's between us
Like two tributaries that come
Together to form one Nile
The two of us can come
Together to form one child
And if this topic
Is too explicit I still can't stop it

Because you and me, see we

Can breed the seed of the prophet

And I don't want to miss this chance

To bring the whole world together

Because this dance this romance

Can enhance forever

So let's enjoy today

So we can look forward to tomorrow

And let me take away

Yesterday's pains and memories of sorrow

Nous pouvons ecrire un nouveau

Livre de l'amour

Avec vous

Comme le petit fleur

Et je comme

Le gardner persistant

Comme nous aimons un

Un autre sans resistant

And you may ask why

Je parle en francais

It's just I want the words I say today

To be half as beautiful as you are everyday

Love to fly

I don't even have to look
To see the god in you
I just close my eyes it ain't hard to do
Though life's lessons has left
My heart scarred it's true
But through this moment in time
I'll make a new start with you
We can come together
For a new beginning
And not worry for we
Can write our own ending
Bending time and space
So that uneasy memories are replaced
With sunshine and roses
Writing lines in a book that never closes and erases

Our mistakes as if
They never happened and make up
Like there's no tomorrow
And all mornings are beautiful when I wake up
With you and we
Can spend the day with the sun's rays
Peeking through the window
Tell you I love you with no words to say
And the only sounds we make
Are those of passionate throes
Natural scents fill our nose
Curling our toes and our love flows
In rivers that never end
Volcanoes erupting again and
Over again and then
It seems like hours we spend
Building rebuilding
Restarting this thing we began
So take the hand
Of your man and understand
That we
Only need our love to fly
Touch the sky
Let me take you up so high

We can sing with the angels

Look over the world below

Come back down

Sneak kisses in mountain valleys so low

We need to rest again

So let me rest in you

Till the end of time

Because I have found my best in you

Déjà vu

Through the eyes you
Remind me of a love I once knew
Back in the days
When I
Used to
Live life so carefree
And easy
But now life's journeys
Takes me
Across stormy seas
To strange countries
And that love
Is all but forgotten
It comes to me
Every now and then when days are hot and

Fades away with summer days
When nights become so long and so cold
And though to me your eyes are new
They remind me of old
And you may
Just say it's insane
But for real
You seem to laugh the same
And these strange places
With all the strange drinks
Seeing all these strange faces
May affect how I think
But you seem
To walk like her
And when you talk
You talk like her
See I can't be sure
But I think her
Smile
Is just the same as yours
You bat your eyes the same
Is it so insane
To think you two
Could be one in the same

Could you be
One that has not changed
Or are you not the same
And into her you have changed
Or could we
Have been on different journeys to the same place
And I am so blessed
To have been returned to the same face
Or maybe
My memory really is just a fantasy
Or have I foreseen this
Because it is simply my destiny
And you are the woman of my dreams
And the dreams just seem
More real than the movie screens
Or maybe
There is no thing called déjà vu
And I am here
With my mind wandering just the same as you
Thinking of old
Or imagined loves as new
Yet for some reason
I feel that if I talk to you
I'll find your first name
Is the same with the last one changed
And it might be strange
But I don't think I would feel the same

Loving Her

The first time I saw you
Your beauty blinded me so much that I
Thought the sun
Had moved inside see my eyes
Are not wide enough
To encompass the blessings of your presence
So like the three wise men
I bring you three presents
My mind
Which is consumed with thoughts of thee
My heart
Which is yours eternally
And
To complete the trinity
My soul
Because eternally I want to be with thee

And fulfilling your hearts desire

Is my life's only purpose

And I will work to give you my last dime

Because there's no price on your loves worth

But if I am only to be your god atlas

Then I shall hold up your world

And write legends of you

As your life story unfurls

Like the Sphinx

I will patiently wait by your side as you sleep

Divert the river Nile

Ask Jesus to bless the water so I can wash your feet

Cut down the mountains

If only to ease your path

Lay down my jacket over a puddle and if

It's too deep you can use my body as a raft

If it's not too much

I will sing you Solomon's song

As you drift along

And if I am ever wrong

And not worthy of your love

Then I will lay down my life

If I ever displease you

I will reach back for my own knife

Cut out my heart
And serve it to you in the Holy Grail
And if by anyone
Your honor is ever assailed
I will come back from the grave
And you can be sure that they'll be slain
Because even in death
In your service I shall remain
And if you're ever harmed
Whether by armies or just one
Red with their blood
The streets shall run
If they speak your name in vain
 I shall cut out their tongue
And if you're ever too hot
I will douse the flames of the sun
And go forbid you go before me
Search for you I will till the call me a fool
I will look for you love forever
Like Lord Vlad of the Dracul
I will breathe life into you
Until I have no life left
I will battle heaven and hell
For your return until my death

And when I go out in flames
History may write my name
For tales of fame
And when barely a memory of me remains
There'll be one thing
They can say for sure
That he was born for her
He loved and lived for her
And in the end
He died
Loving her

Will you

Will you

Show complacency towards my idiosyncrasies

And drive yourself crazy

Just to be in sync with me

I want you to blink

Opposite of me

So the things I miss

You can see

And independently

We can deal with our co dependencies

But I need to know will you

Tend to all my tendencies

And I need one I can be addicted to

So will you feed my addiction

And see these flaws are part of me

And they need no fixing

So we can lie in the bed till noon
And argue about who's lazier
And you say I'm crazy
But you know you're crazier
And you come back and say
That I am the craziest
Well maybe
But baby you know you're the laziest
And we can raid the fridge at midday
For all of its leftovers
And make love until nightfall
With no energy leftover
And you say I crept over
To your side of my king size
But not care
Because I gave till I made your eyes wide
Shut
As we fall into another deep slumber
And when I wake I smile
Because I'm with my number
One through infinity
And you are like wind to me
I breathe in
And only win when you win with me

So will you

Wash away my pride like ocean tides

And make me forget bout

Nights I cried and turn my insides

Out

Like merry go rounds will you make my head spin

Turn my world upside down

And all my frowns to grins

Will you make me see stars in the daytime

And the sun in the night skies

And make my heart feel

Like it lives on mountain highs

And take away

Each and every one of my valley lows

And we can watch our troubles go

As the water flows

Downstream and we

Can live upstream

And love one another

And be lost in each other like daydreams

But only if you

Will be into me like you

Want me

To be so into you

Because I want to come home to you

I want to be home to you

And I want to live the rest of my life

Alone with you

And you say I'm crazy

But will you be crazy with me

And when I miss you

As soon as I leave will you miss me

And when I say I love you

Will you say you love me more

And will you

Be the one I carry through honeymoon doors

Now I know you can't make these promises

And I don't want you to lie

But all of these things I said

Will you

At least try

Acknowledgments

I would like to give thanks to those that have inspired me, encouraged me and gave me an outlet to express my thoughts and feelings.

Ceisha Pardue, Frances Dickens and Shenita Jones who listened to me recite and practice my poetry.
Joeseph Briggs (a.k.a. 1-Wise African) for providing the Fountain of Truth spoken word forum and letting me perform in front of an audience and encouraging me to continue when I have wanted to quit.
Lamont Carey and Komplex and all the other incredibly dynamic performers at The Fountain of Truth for compelling me to continue improving my writing.
To my friends Marvin, Marcus, Marilyn and Ricky for always being there.
To my parents for taking the time to raise me right and instilling a sense of purpose.
To my daughter who keeps me on a straightened path and reminds me of the lessons I try to teach her.
To God.
And most of all to the source of my inspiration for these writings and the title of this collection.

www.ingramcontent.com/pod-product-compliance
Lightning Source LLC
Chambersburg PA
CBHW030142170426

43199CB00008B/177